RONA MUNRO

Rona was born in Aberdeen and has written extensively for stage, film, radio and television. Theatre credits include *Little Eagles* (Hampstead Theatre for the Royal Shakespeare Company); *Pandas* (Traverse Theatre, Edinburgh); *The House of Bernarda Alba* (National Theatre of Scotland); *The Dirt Under the Carpet* (Paines Plough and Òran Mór); *Long Time Dead* (Paines Plough and Plymouth Theatre Royal); *Strawberries in January* (Traverse Theatre, Edinburgh); *Watership Down* (stage adaptation for the Lyric Theatre, Hammersmith); *Mary Barton* (Royal Exchange, Manchester); *The Indian Boy* (Royal Shakespeare Company); *Iron* (Traverse Theatre, winner of the John Whiting Award); *The Maiden Stone* (Hampstead Theatre and Royal Lyceum Theatre, Edinburgh; Peggy Ramsay Memorial Award Winner); *Gilt* (co-writer); *Bold Girls* (Susan Smith Blackburn Award, Evening Standard Most Promising Playwright Award, Plays International Award, Critics' Circle and Plays and Players Most Promising Playwright Award). Rona has written over twenty-five shows for the touring theatre company The MsFits. Film credits include *Oranges and Sunshine* directed by Jim Loach (See Saw Films/Sixteen Films); *Ladybird Ladybird* directed by Ken Loach (FilmFour/Parallax Pictures Ltd); *Aimee and Jaguar* (Senator Film Production). For television, credits include: *Rehab* (BBC2); *Almost Adult* (Channel 4). Rona wrote five of the plays in the Stanley Baxter Playhouse series for Catherine Bailey Ltd/BBC Radio 4.

Other Titles in this Series

Howard Brenton
ANNE BOLEYN
BERLIN BERTIE
FAUST – PARTS ONE & TWO
after Goethe
IN EXTREMIS
NEVER SO GOOD
PAUL
THE RAGGED TROUSERED
PHILANTHROPISTS *after* Tressell

Caryl Churchill
BLUE HEART
CHURCHILL PLAYS: THREE
CHURCHILL PLAYS: FOUR
CHURCHILL: SHORTS
CLOUD NINE
A DREAM PLAY
after Strindberg
DRUNK ENOUGH TO SAY
I LOVE YOU?
FAR AWAY
HOTEL
ICECREAM
LIGHT SHINING IN
BUCKINGHAMSHIRE
MAD FOREST
A NUMBER
SEVEN JEWISH CHILDREN
THE SKRIKER
THIS IS A CHAIR
THYESTES *after* Seneca
TRAPS

Ariel Dorfman
DEATH AND THE MAIDEN
PURGATORIO
READER
THE RESISTANCE TRILOGY
WIDOWS

Helen Edmundson
ANNA KARENINA *after* Tolstoy
THE CLEARING
CORAM BOY *after* Gavin
GONE TO EARTH *after* Webb
LIFE IS A DREAM *after* Calderón
THE MILL ON THE FLOSS *after* Eliot
MOTHER TERESA IS DEAD
ORESTES *after* Euripides
WAR AND PEACE *after* Tolstoy

Debbie Tucker Green
BORN BAD
DIRTY BUTTERFLY
RANDOM
STONING MARY
TRADE & GENERATIONS

Liz Lochhead
BLOOD AND ICE
DRACULA *after* Stoker
EDUCATING AGNES ('The School
for Wives') *after* Molière
GOOD THINGS
MARY QUEEN OF SCOTS GOT
HER HEAD CHOPPED OFF
MEDEA *after* Euripides
MISERYGUTS ('The Miser')
& TARTUFFE *after* Molière
PERFECT DAYS
THEBANS *after* Euripides & Sophocles

Linda McLean
ANY GIVEN DAY
ONE GOOD BEATING
RIDDANCE
SHIMMER
STRANGERS, BABIES

Joanna Murray-Smith
BOMBSHELLS
THE FEMALE OF THE SPECIES
HONOUR

Rona Munro
THE INDIAN BOY
IRON
THE LAST WITCH
LITTLE EAGLES
LONG TIME DEAD
THE MAIDEN STONE
MARY BARTON *after* Gaskell
PANDAS
STRAWBERRIES IN JANUARY
from de la Chenelière
YOUR TURN TO CLEAN THE STAIR
& FUGUE

Amanda Whittington
BE MY BABY
LADIES' DAY
LADIES DOWN UNDER
SATIN 'N' STEEL

Federico García Lorca

THE HOUSE OF BERNARDA ALBA

a new version translated by

Rona Munro

NICK HERN BOOKS
LONDON
www.nickhernbooks.co.uk

A Nick Hern Book

The House of Bernarda Alba by Federico García Lorca first published in Great Britain in 1999 as a paperback original by Nick Hern Books Limited, 14 Larden Road, London W3 7ST

Reprinted 2001, 2003, 2004, 2006, 2008, 2010 (twice), 2011

La Cas de Bernarda Alba by Federico García Lorca

Cover designed by Ned Hoste

Typeset by Country Setting, Kingsdown, Kent
Printed in the UK by CLE Print Group Ltd, St Ives, Cambs PE27 3LE

A CIP catalogue record for this book is available from the British Library

ISBN 978 1 85459 459 4

Foreword

That Lorca, a homosexual man in a fiercely masculine society should write about suppressed sexuality is not surprising. More extraordinary is the degree to which *The House of Bernarda Alba* transcends its domestic setting, becoming a play about freedom and censorship, about self-expression and its opposites, fear and repression. *The House of Bernarda Alba* was written only a month before Lorca was murdered by the fascists in a purge of intellectuals and artists. This perhaps explains the extraordinary atmosphere of foreboding, the nightmarish sense of there being no escape. The house is not only a domestic prison but a metaphor for a country at war.

By writing about a family and a nation, Lorca shows how the desire to suppress another being (because of our own frustrated hopes) operates at a personal and public level. For Bernarda to allow Adela to know love and sexual fulfilment would be to see the meaninglessness of her own life and know that it has been tragically wasted. We sense that beneath Bernarda's formidable exterior lies the wreckage of a woman who has lived a lonely life without love or pleasure. She cannot bear for her daughters to experience the happiness that she herself has never known.

The play explores an unhappy truth. That those who have been oppressed often in turn become the worst oppressors. They repeat the pattern of their own abuse, only feeling safe when they have power over others. The play is above all a passionate plea for change.

Polly Teale,
Associate Director, Shared Experience Theatre

Translating Lorca

When Polly Teale first approached me to translate *La Casa de Bernarda Alba* I was flattered but initially very uncertain. I hadn't attempted a translation before. I was familiar with the play itself, with only a vague memory of a very bad production years ago at the Edinburgh Festival. When I read it my uncertainty increased. It seemed so relentlessly grim, page after page of weeping, black-shawled women gnawing at each other and moaning about their fate. I found myself longing to give them a good slap and to shout at them to get a life. It was only as I read and re-read the text that another vision of the play started to develop for me. What had initially seemed to be a rather repressive vision of passive and hopeless women emerged as a passionate appeal against repression. If only, the play seems to say, we could love where we chose. If only we could throw off mourning and reclaim our relationship with life. If only we could touch each other openly, not through the bars of a window in the dark . . . If only all the forces of tradition and landed wealth could be relaxed so that the rich could consider more than the future of their acres and the poor could be released from the eternal worry of where the next plate of chick peas was coming from.

Written just before the Spanish Civil War, the play can be seen as a 'photographic documentary' as Lorca described it. It is indeed, a beautifully detailed portrait of life for 'women in the villages of Spain'. It's also a testament of the power of fear to weaken people to the effects of tyranny, as relevant today as it ever was. The women in the play are not victims, their repressed power vibrates through each line like 'a thunderstorm waiting in every room'. But there seems no way for them to escape their fate. They've been robbed of the capacity for hope. Reading the play was a poignant reminder of how precious the power to imagine your own future is, how easily it can be taken from us and how terrible the consequences of that loss can be, personally and politically.

'They took him out and shot him in an olive grove when he was 38.' That was the bald phrase that stuck in my head as I was swithering about whether I was really the right person to attempt this job. Anyone can get run over by a bus at any moment, but I imagine another writer always having the next play in their head, the one that's going to be even better, discover more, push your craft even further. Lorca was robbed of his next play. He never even saw a production of *La Casa de Bernarda Alba*. I was already a year older than he ever got to be. If I needed another reason to attempt the translation that was it. What I gained was the humbling and moving experience of coming to understand the rhythm and power of another writer's language. It's like getting a piggy-back ride up a mountain to a fantastic view. They've done the slog and pain, you get the pure joy of juggling the words that are already there . . . Which is not to say it was a piece of cake. There were times, surrounded by Spanish text, literal translation and several previous interpretive translations when I felt like I was drowning in paper. The sense of responsibility to a dead writer is bad enough but a famous dead writer?? Already beautifully translated into English several times??? Who did I think I was? In the end I trusted to the robustness of the original lines to do the work. My job was to make them as accessible and direct as Lorca had originally intended. Friends tell the story of Lorca running up to them waving pages of the script, delighted with what he'd achieved. 'There's not a drop of poetry!' he's said to have shouted, 'Realism, pure realism!'.

To my eyes the play is full of poetry, but of the spare and powerful kind where one line can carry the weight of several complicated and intense emotions. The language is simple and direct but completely evocative of the humanity it describes. I saw my job to be the preservation of this power and the recreation of the simplicity and directness of the original dialogue. Hopefully I have, at least partially, done justice to this wonderful play.

Rona Munro

THE HOUSE OF BERNARDA ALBA

The House of Bernarda Alba was presented in association with Salisbury Playhouse by Shared Experience Theatre and first opened at the Salisbury Playhouse on 11 March 1999. After touring Guildford, West Yorkshire, Richmond, Oxford, Bath and Liverpool, it opened at the Young Vic Theatre, London, on 18 May 1999 with the following cast:

PONCIA	Gabrielle Reidy
ANGUSTIAS	Sandy McDade
BERNARDA	Sandra Duncan
ADELA	Manda Drew
MARTIRIO	Tanya Ronder
PRUDENCIA/MAID	Carolyn Jones
MARIA JOSEFA	Janet Henfrey
MAGDALENA	Ruth Lass
AMELIA	Victoria Finney

Director Polly Teale
Design Angela Davies
Music Peter Salem
Lighting Tina MacHugh
Company Movement Liz Ranken
Assistant Director Titania Krimpas

ACT ONE

An inner room in BERNARDA*'s house. Church bells are ringing in the distance.*

The SERVANT *enters.*

SERVANT. I've got the pain of those bells right inside my head.

PONCIA *enters, eating bread and sausage.*

PONCIA. Over two hours of gabbling and wailing. There are priests here from all over. The church is looking lovely. At the first response Magdalena fainted.

SERVANT. She's the one who's going to be lonely now.

PONCIA. She's the only one who loved the father. Oh! Thank God we're alone for a moment. I'm going to stuff myself.

SERVANT. If Bernarda sees you . . .

PONCIA. Oh right, she's not eating so she doesn't care if the rest of us drop dead of hunger! Slave driver! Bullying old bitch! I've cheated her. I've opened the sausage jar.

SERVANT. Why don't you give me some for my little girl, Poncia?

PONCIA. Dive in! Grab a handful of chickpeas too. She'll not count them today.

VOICE (*off*). Bernarda!

PONCIA. There's the old woman! Is she locked in alright?

SERVANT. With two turns of the key.

PONCIA. But you have to bolt the cross bar too. She's got fingers like five lock-picks.

VOICE (MARIA JOSEFA). Bernarda!

PONCIA (*calling off*). She's coming! (*To* SERVANT.) Do a good job now. If Bernarda doesn't see a shine on everything she'll pull out the few hairs I've got left.

SERVANT. That woman!

PONCIA. She crushes everything close to her. She could sit on your heart and watch you die a whole year and she'd never drop that frosty smile she wears on her wicked face. Scrub then! Scrub those glasses!

SERVANT. I've got blood on my hands from all my scrubbing.

PONCIA. She's the cleanest, she's the most respectable, she's better than the lot of us. Her poor husband, he was due a good rest.

The bells stop.

SERVANT. Did all the relatives come?

PONCIA. Just hers. His people hate her. They just stopped to see him dead and make the sign of the cross over him.

SERVANT. Are there enough chairs?

PONCIA. Plenty. They can sit on the floor. Since Bernarda's father died nobody's been welcome under this roof. She doesn't want them to see her in her lair. Damn her!

SERVANT. She's been good to you.

PONCIA. Thirty years washing her sheets. Thirty years eating her scraps, nights nursing her coughs, days with my eye squashed to the crack in the door to spy on the neighbours and bring her the stories. In all that time together there have been no secrets between her and me and I say damn her! I'd stick a nail in her eyes.

SERVANT. Listen to you!

PONCIA. But I'm the best bitch she has. I bark when she tells me to, I sink my teeth in the beggars' heels when she sets me at them. My sons work in her fields. Thanks to her they've both earned enough to marry. But one day, one day I'll have had it with her.

SERVANT. And that day?

PONCIA. And *that* day I'll lock myself in a room with her and spit in her face for a whole year. 'Bernarda that's for this, and this for *that*, and this is for the rest!' . . . till she looks like a lizard the little boys have smashed on the stones and that's what she is, her and all her family. Oh no, I don't envy her.

She's stuck with five women, five big, ugly, daughters, and only Angustias, the eldest has any money at all.

SERVANT. Well she's daughter to Bernarda's first husband. As for the rest . . .

PONCIA (*chiming in*). . . . a pile of embroidered lace, a whole heap of petticoats but all they'll inherit is bread and grapes.

SERVANT. That would do me.

PONCIA. All we have is our hands and a hole in the ground at the end.

SERVANT. When you have nothing that's the only land they'll ever let you inherit.

PONCIA (*at cupboard*). There are marks on this glass.

SERVANT. I can't get them off with soap or rag.

The bells ring out.

PONCIA. The last response. I'm going over to listen to it. I love the way that priest sings, in the pater noster, up and up and up, little by little like a pitcher being filled up with water. It cracked in the end of course but it's glorious to hear him. Still we'll never hear the like of the old sacristan Tonchapinos, he sang at my mother's mass, God rest her. The walls trembled and his 'Amen' was like a wolf running through the church. (*Imitating it.*) A-a-a-a-men! (*She starts coughing.*)

SERVANT. You'll be swallowing dust!

PONCIA. I'd rather swallow something else. (*She exits, laughing.*)

The SERVANT *cleans, the bells ring out.*

SERVANT. Ding, ding, dong. May God forgive him.

BEGGAR (*coming on with a child*). Blessed be God.

SERVANT. Ding, ding, dong. Let's hope he won't call us for a few years! Ding, ding, dong.

BEGGAR (*louder, getting irritated*). Blessed be God.

SERVANT (*annoyed*). For ever and ever.

BEGGAR. I came for the scraps.

The bells stop.

SERVANT. The gate's that way. Today's scraps are for me.

BEGGAR. Missus, you've got someone looking after you. Me and my daughter are on our own.

SERVANT. So are the dogs and they live.

BEGGAR. They always give them to me.

SERVANT. Get out of here! Who let you in? You'll make dirty footprints all over the floor!

They leave, the SERVANT *goes on scrubbing.*

SERVANT. Floors I've shined up with oil, their cupboards, their ornaments, their iron beds . . . What do we have? A mud hut, a plate full of bitterness and one spoon to eat it with. I pray for the day no one has *that* story to tell. (*The bells ring again.*) Oh yes! Ring those bells, bring out the wooden box with its gold trim and carry it with silken ropes. You'll still come to the same end as me. You're in the mud now, like the rest of us. Suffer it Antonio Maria Benavides, stiff in your hand-made suit and your high boots, *suffer* it! You'll never get your hand up my skirts behind the corral again.

A crowd of WOMEN *in mourning enter in pairs. They wear black shawls and skirts and carry black fans. They enter slowly until the stage is full.*

SERVANT (*breaking into a wail*). Ay! Antonio Maria Benavides. You'll never see these rooms or taste bread here again. I was your best servant. I loved you the most. How can I live without you? How can I live?

The mourners finish coming in, BERNARDA *enters with her five* DAUGHTERS.

BERNARDA (*to the* SERVANT). Be quiet!

SERVANT (*crying*). Yes, Bernarda.

BERNARDA. Less snivelling and more scrubbing. You should have had all this clean for the wake. Get out. This isn't your place.

The MAID *exits, crying.*

BERNARDA. The poor are like animals. It's as if they're made of different stuff.

WOMAN 1. The poor feel their sorrows too.

BERNARDA. And they forget them all in front of a plate of chick peas.

WOMAN 2 (*shyly*). We all have to eat.

BERNARDA. You shouldn't talk like that in front of your elders.

WOMAN 1. Be quiet girl!

BERNARDA. No one lectures me in my own house. Sit down.

They all sit.

BERNARDA. Stop crying Magdalena. If you want to cry go and get under your bed. Do you hear me?

WOMAN 3 (*to* BERNARDA). Have you started your harvest?

BERNARDA. Yesterday.

WOMAN 2. The sun hits like lead out there.

WOMAN 1. I haven't felt heat like this for years.

Pause, they all fan themselves.

BERNARDA. Is the lemonade ready?

PONCIA. Yes, Bernarda.

She brings on a large tray full of little white jars which she hands out.

BERNARDA. Give some to the men.

PONCIA. They're already drinking it in the courtyard.

BERNARDA. And they can leave by the courtyard too. I'm not having them tramping through here.

WOMAN 2 (*to* ANGUSTIAS). Pepe el Romano was with the men in church.

ANGUSTIAS. Yes, he was.

BERNARDA. His mother was! She saw his mother. Neither of us saw Pepe.

WOMAN 2. I thought . . .

BERNARDA. Darajali was there, the widower, very close to your aunt. We all saw him.

WOMAN 3 (*aside*). Oh she's wicked. She's worse than wicked.

WOMAN 1 (*aside*). Tongue like a razor!

BERNARDA. Women in church shouldn't look at any man but the priest. He's safe in his skirts. Women who turn their heads are just looking for a pair of warm trousers.

WOMAN 3 (*quiet*). Old boiled lizard!

PONCIA (*through her teeth*). She's twisted up in knots wanting it herself.

BERNARDA. Praise be to God!

ALL (*crossing themselves*). Blessed and praised for ever.

BERNARDA. Rest in peace with heavenly host around your head.

ALL. Rest in peace.

BERNARDA. With the Archangel Michael and his sword of justice.

ALL. Rest in peace.

BERNARDA. With the key that opens all and the hand that closes all.

ALL. Rest in peace.

BERNARDA. With all the blessed ones and the little lights of the fields.

ALL. Rest in peace.

BERNARDA. With our holy charity and all souls on land or sea.

ALL. Rest in peace.

BERNARDA. Grant peace to your servant Antonio Maria Benavides and give him the crown of your blessed glory.

ALL. Amen.

BERNARDA (*standing and singing*). 'Requiem aeternam dona eis, Domine.

ALL (*also standing and singing the Gregorian way*). 'Et lux perpetua luceat eis'. (*They cross themselves.*)

WOMAN 1. Health to pray for his soul. (*Starting to leave.*)

WOMAN 2. May you never want for warm bread.

WOMAN 3. Or a roof over your daughters' heads.

The mourners are filing out, ANGUSTIAS *leaves by another door, the door into the courtyard.*

WOMAN 1. May you keep all the wealth you had as a wife.

PONCIA (*enters, carrying a bag*). It's from the men, a bag of money to pay for the masses.

WOMAN 2 (*to* MAGDALENA). Magdalena.

MAGDALENA *starts crying.*

BERNARDA (*to* MAGDALENA). Shhhhhh! (*After the departing mourners.*) Go back to your holes and tear me to pieces. I hope it'll be years before any of you pass under the archway of my gate again.

PONCIA. You can't complain. The whole village came.

BERNARDA. Yes, to fill my house with the smell of their sweaty underwear and the poison of their tongues.

AMELIA. Mother, don't talk like that!

BERNARDA. What else can you say about this desert of a place? A village without a river where you daren't dip your tongue in the well water in case it's poisoned.

PONCIA. Look at the state of the floor!

BERNARDA. Looks as if a herd of goats has run over it. (PONCIA *cleans the floor.*) Give me a fan, girl.

ADELA. Here.

She offers her a round fan decorated with red and green flowers. BERNARDA *throws it on the floor.*

BERNARDA. What kind of fan is that to offer a widow? Give me a black one and show some respect to your dead father.

MARTIRIO. Take mine.

BERNARDA. What about you?

MARTIRIO. I don't feel the heat.

BERNARDA. Well get another one, you'll need it. There are eight years of mourning ahead of us. Not even the wind will get into this house. It'll be as if we'd bricked up every window and door. That's how it was in my father's house and my grandfather's. In the meantime you can all start embroidering your trousseaus. I have twenty bolts of linen in the chest to cut up for sheets and bedspreads. Magdalena will embroider them.

MAGDALENA (*sarcastic*). Oh will I?

ADELA (*sourly*). If you don't want to embroider them, they won't get embroidered. Then yours will look better. Is that the idea?

MAGDALENA. *I* don't want to embroider any of them. I know I'm never getting married. I'd rather carry sacks to the mill. I'd rather do anything than sit in this dark room day after day.

BERNARDA. Now you know what it means to be a woman.

MAGDALENA. Yes,we're all cursed.

BERNARDA. In here you'll do what *I* say. You can't go running to your father now. A needle and a thread for the women. A whip and a mule for the men. That's how it should be for a well bred family.

ADELA *exits.*

VOICE. Bernarda! Let me out!

BERNARDA (*calling*). Let her out now!

The SERVANT *enters.*

SERVANT. I could hardly hold her. Your mother may be eighty, but she's as strong as an oak.

BERNARDA. It runs in the family. My grandmother was the same.

SERVANT. I had to stuff an old sack in her mouth every five minutes during the service. She kept shouting for you to bring her dish water and dog food. That's what she says you feed her.

MARTIRIO. She just wants to make trouble.

BERNARDA (*to* SERVANT). She can work it off out in the courtyard.

SERVANT. She took her rings and her amethyst earrings out of her box. She's put them on and now she says she's getting married.

The DAUGHTERS *laugh.*

BERNARDA. Go out with her. Make sure she doesn't go near the well.

SERVANT. You needn't worry. She won't jump in.

BERNARDA. It's not that. The neighbours would see her from their windows.

The SERVANT *exits.*

MARTIRIO. We're going to change.

BERNARDA. Alright, but you keep mourning clothes on your backs.

ADELA *enters.*

BERNARDA. Where's Angustias?

ADELA (*pointedly*). I saw her looking through the cracks in the door. The men had just left.

BERNARDA. And what were you doing at the door?

ADELA. I went to see if the hens had laid.

BERNARDA. The men have left already have they?

ADELA. A group of them were still standing outside.

BERNARDA (*calling, furious*). Angustias! Angustias!

ANGUSTIAS (*entering*). What is it?

BERNARDA. What were you looking at? *Who* were you looking at?

ANGUSTIAS. Nothing. No one.

BERNARDA. Do you think it's decent for a woman of your class to be trailing herself like bait under a man's nose the very day of her father's funeral? Well? Answer me!? Who were you looking at!?

ANGUSTIAS. I . . .

BERNARDA. Yes! You!

ANGUSTIAS. No one.

BERNARDA *steps forward and hits her.*

BERNARDA. Oh you poisonous bit of sugar you!

PONCIA. Bernarda! Calm down!

PONCIA *holds* BERNARDA *back*. ANGUSTIAS *cries*.

BERNARDA. Get out! All of you!

They exit.

PONCIA. She didn't realise what she was doing, that's the worst of it. I couldn't believe it when I saw her sneaking out to the courtyard. Then she stood beside the window listening to the men talking. Of course the conversation wasn't fit for anyone to hear.

BERNARDA. And at a funeral too. (*With curiosity.*) What were they saying?

PONCIA. They were talking about Paca la Rosetta. Last night they tied her husband up in the stable and carried her off on horseback to the top of the olive grove.

BERNARDA. And she let them?

PONCIA. Oh, she loved it. They say her tits were hanging out and Maximillian was holding her like he was playing a guitar. Terrible, eh?

BERNARDA. And what happened then?

PONCIA. What do you think happened then? They came back at dawn. Paca la Rosetta's hair was all over the place and she had a crown of flowers on her head.

BERNARDA. She's the only really bad woman we have in the village.

PONCIA. It's because she's not from around here. She's from a long way off. And the men who went with her are the sons of outsiders too. The men around here couldn't do that.

BERNARDA. No, but they love to see it, and talk about it and suck the gossip off their fingers like gravy.

PONCIA. Oh they were saying more than that.

BERNARDA (*looking round apprehensively*). What?

PONCIA. I'd blush to repeat it Bernarda.

BERNARDA. And my daughter heard this?

PONCIA. That's what I'm telling you!

BERNARDA. That one takes after her aunts, pale and slippery, batting her eyelashes if a hairdresser gives her a compliment. Oh, how I suffer and fight to keep this family under control, to keep them *decent!*

PONCIA. It's because all your daughters are old enough to be married. They don't give you much trouble considering. Angustias must be pushing forty now.

BERNARDA. Thirty-nine.

PONCIA. Think about it. And she's never had a man . . .

BERNARDA (*furious*). None of them has had a man and none of them needs one! They get along fine without one!

PONCIA. I didn't mean to upset you.

BERNARDA. There's no one for a hundred miles who's good enough to come near them. The men here are not of their class. Do you want me to throw them away on some farm hand?

PONCIA. You should've gone to another village.

BERNARDA. I see! To sell them off?

PONCIA. No Bernarda, for the change . . . Of course in a bigger town they wouldn't look so classy.

BERNARDA. Hold your wicked tongue.

PONCIA. I can't talk to you. Do you trust my judgement or not?

BERNARDA. No. You're my servant. I pay you. That's it.

SERVANT (*entering*). Don Arturo is here. He's come to talk about the will.

BERNARDA. Let's go. (*To the* SERVANT.) You can start whitewashing the courtyard. (*To* PONCIA.) And you can start putting the dead man's clothes away.

PONCIA. We could give some of them away . . .

BERNARDA. No! Not even one button. Not even the handkerchief we covered his face with.

She goes out slowly, turning to look at the two MAIDS, *they exit after her.* AMELIA *and* MARTIRIO *enter.*

AMELIA. Did you take your medicine?

MARTIRIO. For all the good it'll do me.

AMELIA. But you took it.

MARTIRIO. I've no faith in things but I do them anyway, like a machine.

AMELIA. You look livelier since the new doctor came.

MARTIRIO. I feel just the same.

AMELIA. Adelaida didn't come to the funeral. Did you notice?

MARTIRIO. I knew she wouldn't. Her fiancé doesn't even let her put her head round the door. Time was she was always laughing. Now she doesn't even put powder on her face.

AMELIA. These days you can't tell if it's better to have a fiancé or not.

MARTIRIO. It makes no difference.

AMELIA. It's all the gossip that's the problem. Who could live with it? Adelaida must have had a terrible time.

MARTIRIO. She's frightened of our mother. She's the only one who knows the truth about how Adelaida's father got his land. Every time Adelaida comes here mother sticks that story in her like a knife. Her father killed his first wife's husband in Cuba so he could marry the wife. Then back here he deserted her and ran off with *another* woman who had a daughter. Then he took up with the daughter. That daughter was Adelaida's mother. He married *her* after the second wife went crazy and died.

AMELIA. What a terrible man! Why isn't he locked up?

MARTIRIO. Because men always cover up for each other and nobody can say a word about it.

AMELIA. Anyway none of that is Adelaida's fault.

MARTIRIO. No, but stories repeat themselves. The way I look at it, it's all coming round again. She'll end up like her mother and her grandmother, both of them lovers to the man that fathered her.

AMELIA. It's too much!

MARTIRIO. I think it's better never to look at a man. I've been afraid of them since I was a little girl. I used to see them in the corral, yoking the oxen and heaving sacks of grain, shouting and stamping their feet on the floor and I'd think . . . imagine being a grown woman, then imagine if a man suddenly flung his arms around you . . . Of course God made me weak and ugly, that'll keep them away from me for ever.

AMELIA. You can't say that! Remember Enrique Humanas? He *really* liked you.

MARTIRIO. Oh so they said! Once I stood all night at my window in my nightdress. He'd let me know through his shepherd's little girl that he was coming . . . but he didn't. It was just talk. And then he married someone else with more money.

AMELIA. And ugly as hell.

MARTIRIO. What do they care about looks? All they care about is land and yokes of oxen and a nice quiet bitch to put their food on the table.

AMELIA. Ouch!

MAGDALENA *enters.*

MAGDALENA. What are you doing?

MARTIRIO. Just sitting.

AMELIA. How about you?

MAGDALENA. Just wandering through the rooms, just for the walk. I've been looking at grandmother's old needlepoint pictures, the woollen dog, the black man wrestling with a lion, we loved them so much when we were little. Those were happy days. A wedding lasted ten days and poisonous tongues weren't in fashion yet. Today we're all so sophisticated, brides wear white veils just like they do in the towns and we drink wine out of bottles but we're rotting away with the fear of what people might say.

MARTIRIO. Only God knew what was coming to us.

AMELIA (*to* MAGDALENA). One of your shoelaces is untied.

MAGDALENA. So what!

AMELIA. You'll trip over it.

MAGDALENA. So? One less.

MARTIRIO. Where's Adela?

MAGDALENA. She put on that green dress she made to wear on her birthday and she went out into the corral and started shouting, 'Chickens! Chickens look at me!' I had to laugh.

AMELIA. If mother had seen her!

MAGDALENA. Poor little thing. She's the youngest of all of us and she still has her daydreams. I'd give a lot to see her happy.

Pause. ANGUSTIAS *crosses the stage, carrying some towels in her hands.*

ANGUSTIAS. What time is it?

MAGDALENA. It must be twelve.

ANGUSTIAS. That late?

AMELIA. It'll strike in a minute.

ANGUSTIAS *goes out.*

MAGDALENA (*meaningfully*). Have you heard?((*pointing after* ANGUSTIAS.)

AMELIA. No.

MAGDALENA. Oh come on!

MARTIRIO. I don't know what you're talking about.

MAGDALENA. You two know better than I do. You've always got your heads together like two little sheep, never letting anyone else in on the secret. About Pepe El Romano!

MARTIRIO. Oh!

MAGDALENA (*mocking her*). Oh! The whole village is talking about it. Pepe el Romano's coming to marry Angustias. Last night he was prowling around the house and I think he's going to send a message soon.

MARTIRIO. Well I'm glad. He's a good man.

AMELIA. Me too. Angustias deserves it.

MAGDALENA. Neither of you is glad.

MARTIRIO. Magdalena! You bitch!

MAGDALENA. If he wanted Angustias for her looks, Angustias the woman, I'd be glad but he's coming for her money. Alright, she's our sister but we're all family here. We know she's old, she's ill and she's the ugliest of the lot of us. If she looked like a stick in a skirt when she was twenty what's she like now she's forty?

MARTIRIO. Don't talk like that. Maybe luck comes to those who're not looking for it.

AMELIA. But she's only telling the truth after all. Angustias has her father's money. She's the only rich woman in the house. So now our father's dead and she'll come into her inheritance. That's why they're after her.

MAGDALENA. Pepe el Romano is twenty-five years old and the best looking man for miles. It'd be natural if he was courting you Amelia, or our Adela. She's only twenty. But to go poking in the darkest shadows in the house, pulling out an old woman who speaks through her nose like her father did . . .

MARTIRIO. Well maybe that's what he likes!

MAGDALENA. You're so two faced Martirio!

MARTIRIO. Oh for the love of God . . . !

ADELA *enters.*

MAGDALENA. Have the chickens seen you yet?

ADELA. Have I missed anything?

AMELIA. If Mother sees you she'll tear your hair out.

ADELA. I've been dreaming about this dress. I was going to wear it the day we go to pick watermelons by the water wheel. There wouldn't have been another like it.

MARTIRIO. It's a beautiful dress.

ADELA. And it suits me so well. It's the best dress Magdalena has ever cut out.

MAGDALENA. What did the chickens say about it?

ADELA. Oh they gave me a few of the fleas that are eating holes in my legs.

They laugh.

MARTIRIO. The best thing you can do is dye it black.

MAGDALENA. The best thing you can do is give it to Angustias for her wedding with Pepe el Romano.

ADELA (*with hidden emotion*). But Pepe el Romano . . .

AMELIA. Haven't you heard about it?

ADELA. No.

MAGDALENA. Well, now you know!

ADELA. It's not possible.

MAGDALENA. Money makes anything possible.

ADELA. Is that why she was following the mourners and spying through the door? (*Pause.*) But how could *he . . . ?*

MAGDALENA. Oh he'll manage.

Pause.

MARTIRIO. What are you thinking Adela?

ADELA. I'm thinking this mourning has caught me at the worst moment in my life. I can't bear it!

MAGDALENA. You'll get used to it.

ADELA. I won't get used to it! I can't be locked up! I don't want my flesh to fade like yours has. I don't want my whiteness lost in these rooms! Tomorrow I'm going to put on my green dress and I'm going to go walk in the streets. I want to go out!

The SERVANT *enters.*

MAGDALENA (*commanding*). Adela!

SERVANT. Oh the poor child, how she misses her father. (*Exits.*)

MARTIRIO. Shut up!

AMELIA. We're all in the same boat Adela.

ADELA *calms down.*

MAGDALENA. The maid nearly heard you!

The SERVANT *enters.*

SERVANT. Pepe el Romano's going past the end of the street.

AMELIA, MARTIRIO *and* MAGDALENA *run off.*

MAGDALENA. Let's go and see him!

SERVANT (*to* ADELA). Aren't you going?

ADELA. I don't care.

SERVANT. He has to turn the corner in a minute. You'll see him better from your bedroom window. (*Exits.*)

ADELA *is left alone, she hesitates then moves quickly towards her bedroom.* BERNARDA *and* PONCIA *come on.*

BERNARDA. Damn that will!

PONCIA. It's such a lot of money for Angustias.

BERNARDA. Yes.

PONCIA. But so much less for the others.

BERNARDA. You've told me that three times already. I'm not talking about it any more. 'Much less, a lot less.' Alright! Don't go on about it!

ANGUSTIAS *comes on, her face is heavily made up.*

BERNARDA. Angustias!

ANGUSTIAS. Mother.

BERNARDA. How dare you powder your face! How dare you even wash your face on the day of your father's funeral!

ANGUSTIAS. He wasn't my father. Mine died a long time ago. Have you forgotten that already?

BERNARDA. Well you owe this man, your sisters' father, more than your own. Thanks to this man, your fortune is intact.

ANGUSTIAS. We'll see about that.

BERNARDA. If only for decency's sake! For respect!

ANGUSTIAS. Mother, let me go out.

BERNARDA. Go out! After I've scraped that powder off your face. You two faced little tart! You're the image of your aunts.

She wipes the make up off ANGUSTIAS*'s face roughly with her handkerchief.*

BERNARDA. Now get out!

PONCIA. Bernarda, don't be so hard on her.

BERNARDA. My mother may be mad but I still have all five senses and I know what I'm doing.

The other DAUGHTERS *enter.*

MAGDALENA. What's going on?

BERNARDA. Nothing's going on.

MAGDALENA (*to* ANGUSTIAS). If you're fighting over the inheritance, you're the richest one anyway. You might as well take the lot.

ANGUSTIAS. Keep your tongue in its hole.

BERNARDA (*beating on the floor*). You think you can do what you like in front of me?! Don't fool yourselves. I'm in charge here until they carry me out feet first!

There are voices off. MARIA JOSEFA, BERNARDA*'s mother enters. She is very old and has put flowers in her hair and at her breast.*

MARIA JOSEFA. Bernarda, where is my mantilla? Nothing I have is going to any of you. Not my rings, not my black moiré dress. Because none of you will get married. Not one of you! Bernarda, give me my pearl necklace!

BERNARDA (*to the* SERVANT). Why did you let her in here?

SERVANT. She got away from me.

MARIA JOSEFA. I ran away because I want to get married, because I want to marry a beautiful man from the shores of the sea. All the men here run away from women.

BERNARDA. Be quiet mother!

MARIA JOSEFA. I won't be quiet! I don't want to watch all these spinsters longing for marriage, turning their hearts into dust. I want to go home Bernarda. I want a man. I want to get married and be happy.

BERNARDA. Lock her up!

MARIA JOSEFA. Let me go Bernarda!

The SERVANT *grabs* MARIA JOSEFA.

BERNARDA. Help her! All of you!

They all take hold of the old woman.

MARIA JOSEFA. I want to get away Bernarda! I want to get married beside the sea, beside the sea!

Quick curtain.

ACT TWO

A white room in BERNARDA*'s house. The doors to the left lead to the bedrooms.* BERNARDA*'s* DAUGHTERS *are seated on low chairs, sewing.* MAGDALENA *is embroidering.* PONCIA *is with them.*

ANGUSTIAS. That's the third sheet cut out.

MARTIRIO. That one's for Amelia.

MAGDALENA. Should I put Pepe's initials on this, Angustias?

ANGUSTIAS (*dryly*). No.

MAGDALENA (*calling off*). Adela, aren't you coming?

AMELIA. She'll be lying in bed.

PONCIA. There's something up with that one. She's restless, shaking as if she's terrified or she's got a lizard between her tits.

MARTIRIO. There's nothing wrong with her that isn't wrong with all of us.

MAGDALENA. All of us except Angustias.

ANGUSTIAS. Yes, I feel great. If it's upsetting you, you can go chase yourself.

MAGDALENA. I always thought your best features were your tiny little waist and your *lovely* manners Angustias.

ANGUSTIAS. Thank God I'll soon be out of this hell hole.

MAGDALENA. But maybe you won't.

MARTIRIO. Change the subject!

ANGUSTIAS. When it comes down to it a pile of gold in your bottom drawer will get you far more than a pair of dark eyes in your face.

MAGDALENA. In one ear and out the other.

AMELIA (*to* PONCIA). Open the door onto the courtyard will you? Let's see if we can get some air in here.

The SERVANT *opens the door.*

MARTIRIO. I couldn't sleep last night because of the heat.

AMELIA. Neither could I.

MAGDALENA. I got up to cool off. There was a great black storm cloud. A few drops of rain did fall.

PONCIA. It was one in the morning and the earth was still on fire. I got up too. Angustias was still at the window with Pepe.

MAGDALENA (*ironically*). That late? What time did he leave?

ANGUSTIAS. Magdalena, why ask if you saw him?

AMELIA. He must have left about half one.

ANGUSTIAS. Yes? How do you know?

AMELIA. I heard him cough and heard his mare's hooves.

PONCIA. But I heard him leave about four.

ANGUSTIAS. It can't have been him.

PONCIA. I'm sure it was.

MARTIRIO. That's what I thought too.

MAGDALENA. That's very strange.

Pause.

PONCIA. Hey Angustias, what did he say to you the first time he came to your window?

ANGUSTIAS. Nothing! What should he say? Just small talk.

MARTIRIO. Isn't it strange that two people who don't know each other can meet at the bars of a window and next thing they're engaged?

ANGUSTIAS. I didn't find it strange.

AMELIA. I don't know what I would have felt.

ANGUSTIAS. But when a man comes to the window he already knows from all the people who've been in and out of the house, fetching and carrying, that you'll say yes.

MARTIRIO. Alright, but he should still ask you.

ANGUSTIAS. Of course!

AMELIA (*with curiosity*). What did he say?

ANGUSTIAS. Oh nothing much . . . 'You know I'm asking for you. I need a good, decent woman. That's you, if you agree.'

AMELIA. Oh it's so embarrassing!

ANGUSTIAS. Yes, but you have to go through it.

PONCIA. Did he say anything else?

ANGUSTIAS. He did all the talking.

MARTIRIO. What about you?

ANGUSTIAS. I couldn't have said a word. My heart was almost coming out my mouth. It was the first time I was ever alone with a man at night.

MAGDALENA. And such a good looking man.

ANGUSTIAS. He's not bad.

PONCIA. That's how it is with an educated man, someone who can talk up a storm and wave his hands about . . . The first time *my* husband, Evaristo el Colin came to my window . . . (*Starts to laugh.*)

AMELIA. What happened?

PONCIA. It was very dark. I saw him going by and he said, 'Good evening'. 'Good evening' I said, and then we both just stood there, silent, for half an hour or more. The sweat was running down my body. Then Evaristo got nearer and nearer as if he wanted to squeeze in through the bars and in a low, low voice he said 'Come here! Let me feel you!'

They all laugh, AMELIA *gets up and runs to peer out the door.*

AMELIA. I thought I heard mother coming!

MAGDALENA. She'd've had something to say to us!

They go on laughing.

AMELIA. Shhhh! She'll hear us!

PONCIA. Afterwards, he behaved himself. Instead of getting other ideas he took to breeding linnets until he died. You single girls should listen to this, it'll be good for you. Fifteen days after the wedding the man gives up the bed for the table, then the table for the tavern. The woman who can't put up with that will rot away in her own tears.

AMELIA. You put up with it?

PONCIA. Oh, I could handle him.

MARTIRIO. Is it true you sometimes hit him?

PONCIA. I nearly put his eye out once.

MAGDALENA. That's how all women should be!

PONCIA. I'm made from the same mould as your mother. One day, I don't know what he said to me, anyway I killed all his linnets with a rolling pin.

They laugh.

MAGDALENA. Adela sweetheart, you're missing this.

AMELIA. Adela!

Pause.

MAGDALENA. I'll go and see.

PONCIA. That girl is ill.

MARTIRIO. Of course she is, she hardly sleeps.

PONCIA. So what does she do?

MARTIRIO. How would I know?

PONCIA. You'd know better than me. You sleep just through the wall from her.

ANGUSTIAS. She's eaten up with envy.

AMELIA. Don't exaggerate.

ANGUSTIAS. I can see it in her eyes. She's starting to look like a mad woman.

MARTIRIO. Don't talk about mad women. This is the last place you should mention that word.

MAGDALENA *and* ADELA *enter.*

MAGDALENA. You weren't asleep then?

ADELA. I'm sick.

MARTIRIO (*meaningfully*). Didn't you sleep well last night?

ADELA. Yes.

MARTIRIO. Well then?

ADELA (*loudly*). Leave me alone! Whether I'm sleeping or not, it's none of your business! My health's my concern, no one else's!

MARTIRIO. I was just worrying about you.

ADELA. Worried or just plain nosy? Weren't you sewing? Well why don't you get on with it? I wish I was invisible so I could get through these rooms without everyone asking me where I'm going.

SERVANT (*entering*). Bernarda's calling you. The lace seller's here.

They go out, as MARTIRIO *leaves she looks pointedly at* ADELA.

ADELA. Stop looking at me! Tell you what, I'll give you my beautiful bright eyes and my straight back to fix that hump you're carrying, but stop staring at me every time I walk by!

MARTIRIO *leaves*.

PONCIA. Adela, she's your sister, and she's the one who loves you most.

ADELA. She follows me everywhere. Sometimes she creeps into my room to see if I'm sleeping. And all the time she's going 'Oh Adela, your pretty face, it's such a shame. It's such a shame that lovely body will be wasted.' It's not true. My body is ready for whoever I want.

PONCIA. It's for Pepe el Romano isn't it?

ADELA. What are you saying?

PONCIA. You heard me!

ADELA. Shut up!

PONCIA (*loud*). You think I haven't noticed?

ADELA. Lower your voice.

PONCIA. You'd better change your ideas, right now!

ADELA. What do you know?

PONCIA. Old women like me can see through walls. Where do you go when you get up at night?

ADELA. I hope you go blind.

PONCIA. I've got eyes in my head and my hands when it comes to something like this. But I can't get my head round you. Why were you standing half naked in your window, window wide open, light spilling out into the street . . . Why Adela? I saw you, the second night Pepe came to visit your sister.

ADELA. It's not true!

PONCIA. Grow up Adela. Leave your sister alone and if you want Pepe el Romano, keep it to yourself! Besides, who says you can't marry him? That sister of yours isn't strong. She'll never survive the first baby. She's old and her hips are narrow. I know the signs. She'll die. Then Pepe will do what all widowers do in this place, he'll marry the youngest and the prettiest and that's you. Feed that hope or forget him, whatever you like, but don't go against God's law.

ADELA. Be quiet.

PONCIA. I will not!

ADELA. Mind your own business you spy! You monster!

PONCIA. I'll be your shadow Adela.

ADELA. Instead of cleaning this house and going to bed to pray for your dead, you root around like an old sow, digging up other people's business so you can drool over it.

PONCIA. I watch over this family so that people won't spit when they pass the door!

ADELA. And what a great affection you have for my sister all of a sudden.

PONCIA. I don't feel any loyalty to any of you but I want to live in a decent house! I don't want to be stained with your dirt in my old age.

ADELA. You can keep your advice. You're too late. You're only a servant. I'd leap over you and my mother too, if I had to. I'd do anything to put out the fire that's growing in my legs, in my mouth . . . What tales can you tell her about me? That I lock myself in my room and won't open the door? That I don't sleep? Oh I'm more clever than you! See if you can catch this hare with your bare hands.

PONCIA. Don't defy me Adela! Don't defy me! I can shout. I can light the torches. I can ring the bell.

ADELA. Bring four thousand burning yellow torches and put them all around the walls of the corral. Nobody can stop what's going to happen now.

PONCIA. You want this man that much?

ADELA. And more. When I look in his eyes it's as if I'm slowly drinking his blood.

PONCIA. I can't listen to you.

ADELA. You'll have to! You used to scare me but I'm stronger than you now.

ANGUSTIAS *enters.*

ANGUSTIAS. Arguing as usual!

PONCIA. Of course. She wants me to go to the shops in this heat and bring her I don't know what.

ANGUSTIAS. Did you buy that bottle of perfume for me?

PONCIA. The most expensive one. And the face powder. I've put them on the table in your room.

ANGUSTIAS *goes out.*

ADELA. You won't say a thing about this!

PONCIA. We'll see.

MARTIRIO, MAGDALENA *and* AMELIA *enter.*

MAGDALENA (*to* ADELA). Did you see the lace?

AMELIA. The ones for Angustias's wedding sheets are just beautiful.

MARTIRIO *brings out some lace.*

ADELA. What are those for?

MARTIRIO. That's for me, for a petticoat.

ADELA. I'm glad you've still got your sense of humour.

MARTIRIO. I'll admire myself in it. I don't need to show myself off to anyone.

PONCIA. Who's going to see any of us in our underwear?

MARTIRIO (*looking meaningfully at* ADELA). Oh some of us might get lucky. I love underwear. If I was rich, I'd have it all made of Dutch linen. It's one of the few pleasures I have left.

PONCIA. This lace would be beautiful for babies' caps and christening robes. I could never have used stuff like this for my babes.We'll see if Angustias will have them for hers. If she takes a fancy for having babies, you'll all be sewing day and night.

MAGDALENA. No, I don't think I'll sew a stitch on those clothes.

AMELIA. Or bring up someone else's children. Look at those women down the street, martyrs to four monsters.

PONCIA. They're better off than you. At least they laugh and you can hear them when they argue.

MARTIRIO. So go and work for them.

PONCIA. No. Fate sent me to this convent and here I stay.

Distant bells are heard as if a long way off, through several walls.

MAGDALENA. That's the men going back to work.

PONCIA. It struck three o'clock a minute ago.

MARTIRIO. In this heat!

ADELA (*sitting down*). If only I could get out in the fields too.

MAGDALENA (*sitting down*). Everybody has their place.

MARTIRIO (*sitting down*). That's how it is.

AMELIA (*sitting down*). Ay!

PONCIA. There's nothing like being in the fields at this time of year. The harvesters arrived yesterday morning. Forty or fifty lovely boys.

MAGDALENA. Where are they from this year?

PONCIA. Miles away. They come from the mountains. Happy!? Dark as burnt trees! Shouting and throwing stones! Last night a woman came into the village wearing sequins and dancing with an accordion. Fifteen of them made a deal with her in the olive grove. I was watching from a long way off. The boy who made the deal had green eyes and a tight body like a sheaf of wheat.

AMELIA. Is that true?

ADELA. Of course it is!

PONCIA. Years ago another of those women came and I gave my eldest son money to go to her myself. Men need these things.

ADELA. They get away with everything.

AMELIA. There's nothing worse than being a woman.

MAGDALENA. Even our eyes aren't our own.

A distant song is heard coming nearer.

PONCIA. There they are. They have some beautiful songs.

AMELIA. They're going to reap the fields.

CHORUS.
Ya salen los degadores
en busca de las espigas;
se llevan los corazones
de las muchachas que miran.

Tambourines and carranacas are heard, a pause. All the women are listening in the silence pierced by sunlight.

AMELIA. They don't mind the heat.

MARTIRIO. They're reaping flames.

ADELA. I'd like to be a reaper so I could go wherever I wanted. Then we'd forget what's eating us alive?

MARTIRIO. What do you have to forget?

ADELA. Everyone has their own troubles.

MARTIRIO (*with feeling*). Everyone!

PONCIA. Be quiet! Be quiet!

CHORUS.
Abrir puertas y ventanas
las que vivis en el pueblo
el segador pide rosas
para adornar su sombrero.

PONCIA. What a song!

MARTIRIO *hums the melody,* ADELA *joins in with feeling.*

The song grows more distant.

PONCIA. Now they're turning the corner.

ADELA. Let's go and watch them from my bedroom window.

PONCIA. Careful not to open the shutters too far, they're always ready to give them a push and see who's peeking out.

ADELA, PONCIA *and* MAGDALENA *leave,* MARTIRIO *is left, sitting with her head in her hands.* AMELIA *approaches her.*

AMELIA. What's wrong with you?

MARTIRIO. I'm sick with the heat.

AMELIA. Is that all?

MARTIRIO. I wish it was November, rainy days, frost, anything but this endless summer.

AMELIA. It'll pass and it'll come again.

MARTIRIO. Yes I know! (*Pause.*) What time did you go to sleep last night?

AMELIA. I don't know. I sleep like a log. Why?

MARTIRIO. No reason . . . only I thought I heard someone in the corral.

AMELIA. Yes?

MARTIRIO. Very late.

ADELA. Weren't you scared?

MARTIRIO. No, I've heard it for a few nights now.

AMELIA. We'll have to be careful. Could it have been the workers?

MARTIRIO. The workers start at six.

AMELIA. Perhaps it was one of the young mules that hasn't been broken in.

MARTIRIO (*through her teeth*). Yes, that's it. A young mule that hasn't been broken in.

AMELIA. We better warn the others.

MARTIRIO. No, no. Don't say anything. I might have imagined it.

AMELIA. Maybe.

Pause. AMELIA *starts to leave*.

MARTIRIO. Amelia.

AMELIA (*at the door*). What?

MARTIRIO. Nothing.

Pause.

AMELIA. Why did you call me?

Pause

MARTIRIO. It just came out. I didn't mean to.

Pause.

AMELIA. You should get some rest.

ANGUSTIAS *burst on stage, her manner is in marked contrast to her previous reticence*.

ANGUSTIAS. Where's the picture of Pepe that was under my pillow!? Which one of you took it!?

MARTIRIO. No one.

AMELIA. It's not as if Pepe's a silver icon.

ANGUSTIAS. Where's my picture?!

PONCIA, MAGDALENA *and* ADELA *enter.*

ADELA. What picture?

ANGUSTIAS. One of you has hidden it!

MAGDALENA. You've got a nerve Angustias!

ANGUSTIAS. It was in my room and now it's gone.

MARTIRIO. Maybe it jumped into the corral around midnight. Pepe likes to walk in the moonlight.

ANGUSTIAS. Don't mess with me! When he comes I'm going to tell him!

PONCIA. Don't do that. It'll turn up.

ANGUSTIAS. I want to know which of you has it!

ADELA (*looking at* MARTIRIO). Someone has it. It could be any of us but it isn't me.

MARTIRIO (*pointed*). Oh no, it couldn't be her.

BERNARDA *enters.*

BERNARDA. What's all this noise? There's not another sound in this heavy heat. The neighbours will have their ears glued to the walls.

ANGUSTIAS. They've stolen my fiancé's picture!

BERNARDA (*fiercely*). Who? Who?

ANGUSTIAS. Them!

BERNARDA. Which of you? (*Silence.*) Answer me! (*Silence. To* PONCIA.) Search their rooms, look in their beds. This is what comes of not keeping you on a tighter leash. But the alarm bell is ringing now! (*To* ANGUSTIAS.) Are you sure?

ANGUSTIAS. Yes.

BERNARDA. Have you looked everywhere?

ANGUSTIAS. Yes mother.

They all stand in embarrassed silence.

BERNARDA. So, you wait till I'm old then you make me drink the bitterest poison of all.

PONCIA *comes back.*

BERNARDA. Did you find it?

PONCIA. Here it is.

BERNARDA. Where was it?

PONCIA. It was . . .

BERNARDA. Come on! What are you afraid of?

PONCIA. Between the sheets in Martirio's bed.

BERNARDA (*to* MARTIRIO). Is that true?

MARTIRIO. Yes, it is.

BERNARDA (*moving in on her, hitting her*). I should stab you dead! You're poison. Scattering broken glass for us to walk on!

MARTIRIO (*fierce*). Don't you hit me mother!

BERNARDA. I'll hit you if I want to!

MARTIRIO. If I let you! Do you hear me!? Get away from me!

PONCIA. Show some respect for your mother!

ANGUSTIAS (*holding* BERNARDA). Leave her! Please!

BERNARDA. Look at her! Not a tear in her eyes!

MARTIRIO. I'm not going to cry just to make you happy.

BERNARDA. Why did you take the picture?

MARTIRIO. Can't I even play a joke on my sister? Why else would I want it?

ADELA (*interrupting, jealous*). It wasn't a joke! Since when have you liked jokes? There's something else boiling up inside you, waiting to burst out. Go on! Admit it!

MARTIRIO. Shut up! You want me to speak my mind? Are you sure? If I told half of what I know the walls of this place would fall in on each other with the shame of it!

ADELA. There's no end to the lies an evil tongue can tell.

BERNARDA. Adela!

MAGDALENA. You're both mad.

AMELIA. Throwing your wicked thoughts at us like stones!

MARTIRIO. There are others doing worse than that.

ADELA. Until they're standing there, naked, and the river sweeps them away!

BERNARDA. You shameless hussy!

ANGUSTIAS. It's not my fault Pepe el Romano chose me.

ADELA. Yes, for your money!

ANGUSTIAS. Mother!

BERNARDA. Silence!

MARTIRIO. For your fields and orchards.

MAGDALENA. Isn't that the truth!

BERNARDA. I said silence! I could see this storm coming but I never thought it would break so soon. You've poured hate on my heart like a hail storm. But I'm not so old yet. I've got five chains, one for each of you and these walls my father built to keep you in. Not even the weeds will know of my desolation. Now get out!

They all leave. BERNARDA *sits down, devastated.* PONCIA *is standing by the wall.* BERNARDA *recovers herself and stamps on the floor.*

BERNARDA. I'll have to use my fists! Remember your duty Bernarda!

PONCIA. Can I speak?

BERNARDA. Go ahead. I'm sorry you heard that. That's what comes of letting outsiders into the family.

PONCIA. I've seen what I've seen.

BERNARDA. Angustias has to get married at once.

PONCIA. Yes, we have to get her away from here.

BERNARDA. Not her! Him!

PONCIA. Of course, you have to get *him* away from here. Good thinking.

BERNARDA. I don't *think*. There are some things you must not stop to think about. I give orders.

PONCIA. And do you think he'll want to leave?

BERNARDA. What's going on in that head of yours now?

PONCIA. Well of course he'll marry Angustias.

BERNARDA. Out with it. I know you well enough to see when you're getting your knife ready.

PONCIA. Since when has a warning been the same as murder?

BERNARDA. You want to warn me about something?

PONCIA. I'm not pointing the finger at anyone Bernarda, I'm just telling you to keep your eyes open. Then you'll see.

BERNARDA. See what?

PONCIA. You've always been a smart one. You could smell the wickedness in folk a hundred miles away. I used to think you could read thoughts. But your children are still your children. When it comes to them you're blind.

BERNARDA. You mean Martirio?

PONCIA. Well . . . yes . . . Martirio . . . Why would she hide that picture?

BERNARDA (*covering up*). She said it was a joke. What else could it be?

PONCIA (*scornful*). You think so do you?

BERNARDA (*stern*). I don't *think* so. I know it!

PONCIA. Alright. It's your business. But if you heard all this was happening to your neighbours over the road . . . what would you think then?

BERNARDA. I can see the point of that knife now.

PONCIA (*hard*). No Bernarda, there's something serious happening here. I'm not putting the blame on you but you've never given those girls any freedom. Martirio is sick for love, whatever you say. Why didn't you let her marry Enrique Humanas. Why, on the very day he was to visit her window did you send him a message telling him not to come?

BERNARDA. I'd do the same a thousand times over. I won't mix my blood with the Humanas while there's breath in me. His father was a farm hand.

PONCIA. And just look where those airs and graces have got you!

BERNARDA. I can afford to be choosy! You can't because you know very well where you come from!

PONCIA (*bitter*). Alright, don't rub it in. I'm an old woman, I'm grateful for your protection.

BERNARDA (*hard*). I don't see much gratitude here.

PONCIA (*swallowing her feelings*). Martirio will forget this.

BERNARDA. And if she doesn't, too bad. I don't believe there's 'something serious happening here'. There's nothing going on here. You just wish there was. And let me tell you, if anything ever does, it won't get beyond these four walls.

PONCIA. Don't be so sure. There are plenty others in this village who can smell wickedness hidden a hundred miles away.

BERNARDA. You'd like that wouldn't you? To see me and my daughters on our way to the whorehouse.

PONCIA. No woman can tell how she'll end up.

BERNARDA. I know how me and my daughters will end our days. The whorehouse was the place for a woman you might remember.

PONCIA. You'll show my mother respect!

BERNARDA. Then stop tormenting me with your evil imagination.

PONCIA. I better just stay out of all of this.

BERNARDA. So you should. Do your work and keep your mouth shut. That's your place. That's what you're paid for.

PONCIA. Well I can't! Don't you know it would be better for Pepe to marry Martirio or . . . yes! Adela.

BERNARDA. I don't think so.

PONCIA. Adela is his real fiancé.

BERNARDA. Things don't always turn out the way we want them to.

PONCIA. But there's a natural way for them to go and it's hard work forcing them down another path. It just seems wrong to me for Pepe to be with Angustias. It would seem wrong to anyone, it would seem wrong to the very air we breathe! Who knows if they'll get what they want?

BERNARDA. Here we go again. Sneaking up on me, filling my head with bad dreams. I'm not listening Poncia because if I could hear you I'd rip you open.

PONCIA. Sticks and stones . . .

BERNARDA. Thank God my daughters respect me. They'll never twist against my will.

PONCIA. True, but if you ever loosen your grip they'll fly straight over the rooftops.

BERNARDA. And I'll bring them down with stones.

PONCIA. You're a brave woman Bernarda.

BERNARDA. I've always preferred the hottest pepper.

PONCIA. But isn't life strange? Who would have thought Angustias would have been so taken with her fiancé at her age? And he seems just as keen. Yesterday my eldest boy said they were still talking at 4.30 in the morning when he went past on his oxen.

BERNARDA. At 4.30?

ANGUSTIAS *enters.*

ANGUSTIAS. That's a lie!

PONCIA. That's what he told me.

BERNARDA (*to* ANGUSTIAS). Well?

ANGUSTIAS. For over a week Pepe has been leaving at one in the morning. God strike me dead if I'm lying.

MARTIRIO *enters.*

MARTIRIO. I heard him leaving at four too.

BERNARDA. But did you see him with your own eyes?

MARTIRIO. I wasn't going to lean out the window. (*To* ANGUSTIAS.) You talk to him through the side window onto the street now, don't you?

ANGUSTIAS. No. I talk to him through my bedroom window.

ADELA *enters.*

MARTIRIO. Then . . .

BERNARDA. What's going on here?

PONCIA. Are you sure you want to hear this? Because it's certain Pepe was at *one* of the windows in this house at four in the morning.

BERNARDA. You're certain?

PONCIA. As certain as you can be about anything in this life.

ADELA. Mother don't listen to her, she'd love to see us lose everything.

BERNARDA. I will find out! If the people of this village want to spread their lying tales they'll hit a flint wall. We do not talk about this. Sometimes people try and stir up a wave of mud to drown us.

MARTIRIO. I'm not lying.

PONCIA. Something is going on.

BERNARDA. And it stops here! I was born with my eyes wide open. Now I'll watch without blinking till I die.

ANGUSTIAS. I have a right to know what's going on!

BERNARDA. You don't have any rights except to do what I tell you! No one's above me here. (*To* PONCIA.) And you mind your own business. No one will take one step here but I'll know about it.

The SERVANT *enters.*

SERVANT. There's a big crowd at the top of the street and all the neighbours are at their doors.

BERNARDA (*to* PONCIA). Run out and see what's happening!

All the others start to run out.

BERNARDA. Where are you off to? I always knew you were window watchers, can't wait to break your mourning eh? Get down from there, the lot of you!

They all go out with BERNARDA *except* MARTIRIO *and* ADELA. *Distant shouting is heard.*

MARTIRIO. You're lucky I kept my tongue tied.

ADELA. I could have said plenty myself.

MARTIRIO. What would you have said then? Wanting isn't the same as doing.

ADELA. And the one who does it is the one who can. I got there first. You wanted it alright, but what could you do?

MARTIRIO. You can't go on like this.

ADELA. I can have everything!

MARTIRIO. I'll tear your arms off him.

ADELA. Martirio, leave me alone!

MARTIRIO. Never!

ADELA. He wants me to live with him.

MARTIRIO. I saw what he wanted to do. I saw how he held you.

ADELA. I didn't want to. It's as if I was dragged by a thick rope.

MARTIRIO. I'll finish you first.

MAGDALENA *and* ANGUSTIAS *look in, the noise outside is increasing*. PONCIA *enters with* BERNARDA.

PONCIA. Bernarda!

BERNARDA. What's happening?

PONCIA. Librada's daughter, the unmarried one, she's had a baby and no one knows whose it is.

ADELA. A baby?

PONCIA. And to hide her shame she killed it and buried it under rocks. But some dogs, with more heart than most humans, dug it out again and dragged it to her door as if God himself had guided them. Now the people will kill her. They're dragging her through the streets, down every path, through the olive groves . . . the men are running and shouting till the fields shake.

BERNARDA. Let them all come with olive sticks and pine handles! Let them come and kill her!

ADELA. No, no! Don't kill her! No!

MARTIRIO. Yes! Let's join them!

BERNARDA. Let any woman who drags her honour in the dirt pay the price!

A woman screams off, followed by a great clamour of noise.

ADELA. Let her go! Don't go out there!

MARTIRIO (*looking at* ADELA). Let her pay the price.

BERNARDA (*at the gate*). Finish her before the guard gets here! Shove hot coals up where her sin started!

ADELA (*clutching herself*). No! No!

BERNARDA. Kill her! Kill her!

ACT THREE

The indoor courtyard in BERNARDA*'s house. It is night. The decor must be extremely simple. The doorways, illuminated by the lights inside the rooms, give a dim glow to the courtyard.*

At the centre there is a table with an oil lamp where BERNARDA *and her* DAUGHTERS *are eating.* PONCIA *serves them.* PRUDENCIA *is seated apart. At the start of the scene it is very quiet, only the noises of cutlery on plates.*

PRUDENCIA. I must be going now, I've kept you too long.

BERNARDA. Hold on woman, we hardly ever see each other.

PRUDENCIA. Have they sounded the last call to rosary?

PONCIA. Not yet.

PRUDENCIA *sits down again.*

BERNARDA. How's your husband getting on?

PRUDENCIA. As ever.

BERNARDA. We never see him either.

PRUDENCIA. You know what he's like. Ever since he quarrelled with his brothers over the inheritance he won't use the front door. He takes a ladder and climbs out over the wall by the corral.

BERNARDA. A real man. And how's he getting on with your daughter?

PRUDENCIA. He won't forgive her.

BERNARDA. He's quite right.

PRUDENCIA. Well I don't know, I'm the one who suffers because of it.

BERNARDA. A disobedient daughter is your enemy not your child.

PRUDENCIA. Oh, I let the water flow. The only consolation I have is to take refuge in the church, but I'm losing my sight now. I'll have to stop going out. The children make fun of me.

There's the sound of a heavy blow against the wall.

PRUDENCIA. What was that?

BERNARDA. The stallion. He's locked in his stall. He's kicking against the sides of the house. (*Calls off.*) Tether him and let him out in the yard! He must be hot.

PRUDENCIA. Are you going to put the new mares to him?

BERNARDA. At dawn.

PRUDENCIA. You've really got the knack of building up your stock.

BERNARDA. With a bit of money and a lot of worry.

PONCIA (*cutting in*). She has the best stable for miles around. It's a pity prices are so low.

BERNARDA. Would you like a little cheese and honey?

PRUDENCIA. No thank you. I've no appetite.

There is another blow.

PONCIA. My God!

PRUDENCIA. I felt my heart shaking in my chest!

BERNARDA (*getting up, furious*). Do I have to say everything twice!? Let him out to roll in the straw! (*Pause then, half to herself, half to the stable hands.*) Lock the mares in the corral but let him loose or he'll bring the walls down on our heads. (*She returns to the table and sits down.*) Ay! What a life!

PRUDENCIA. You have to fight like any man.

BERNARDA. Well . . . that's how it is.

ADELA *gets up.*

BERNARDA. Where are you going?

ADELA. To drink some water.

BERNARDA (*calling off*). Bring a jug of cold water! (*To* ADELA.) You can sit down.

ADELA *sits down.*

PRUDENCIA. And when is Angustias getting married?

BERNARDA. They'll be coming to ask for her in the next three days.

PRUDENCIA. You must be so pleased.

BERNARDA. Of course!

AMELIA (*to* MAGDALENA). Now you've spilled the salt.

MAGDALENA. Your luck couldn't get any worse anyway.

AMELIA. It always brings bad luck!

BERNARDA. That's enough!

PRUDENCIA (*to* ANGUSTIAS). Has he given you the ring yet?

ANGUSTIAS (*holding it out*). Have a look.

PRUDENCIA. Oh it's beautiful. Three pearls. Of course in my day pearls meant tears.

ANGUSTIAS. But things have changed now.

ADELA. I don't think so. Things always mean what they mean. Engagement rings should be diamonds.

PRUDENCIA. That would've been better.

BERNARDA. Pearls or not, life's what you make it.

MARTIRIO. Or as God wills.

PRUDENCIA. I've been told the furniture is beautiful.

BERNARDA. It cost me sixteen thousand reales.

PONCIA (*interrupting*). The best is this wardrobe with a mirror.

PRUDENCIA. I've never seen one of those.

BERNARDA. We just had a chest.

PRUDENCIA. Of course what's most important is that everything works out for the best.

ADELA. Because you never know.

BERNARDA. There's no reason why it shouldn't.

Bells are heard in the distance.

PRUDENCIA. The last call. (*To* ANGUSTIAS.) I'll come again so you can show me the wedding clothes.

ANGUSTIAS. Whenever you like.

PRUDENCIA. Good evening and God bless you all.

BERNARDA. Goodbye Prudencia.

ALL DAUGHTERS. God go with you.

Pause. PRUDENCIA *leaves.*

BERNARDA. The meal's over.

They get up.

ADELA. I'm going to walk down to the gate to stretch my legs and get some fresh air.

MAGDALENA *sits down on a low chair and leans against the wall.*

AMELIA. I'll come with you.

MARTIRIO. So will I.

ADELA (*controlling anger*). I don't think I'll get lost.

AMELIA. You need company in the dark.

They all go out. BERNARDA *sits down.* ANGUSTIAS *is clearing the table.*

BERNARDA. I've already told you, I want you to talk to Martirio. That business with the picture was a joke. You should forget it.

ANGUSTIAS. You know she doesn't like me.

BERNARDA. Who knows what's in anyone's head? I'm not going to pry into anyone's heart. I want a good front to the world and peace inside the family. Do you understand?

ANGUSTIAS. Yes.

BERNARDA. Then that's how it is.

MAGDALENA (*half asleep*). Besides, you'll be gone in no time. (*She nods off.*)

ANGUSTIAS. Not soon enough for me.

BERNARDA. What time did you stop talking last night?

ANGUSTIAS. Half past twelve.

BERNARDA. What does Pepe have to say?

ANGUSTIAS. He seems a bit distracted. He talks to me as if he's thinking of something else. If I ask him what's wrong he just says, 'We men have our problems.'

BERNARDA. You shouldn't ask. Definitely not when you're married. You speak when he speaks. You look at him if he looks at you. That way you won't ever fall out.

ANGUSTIAS. Mother, I think he's hiding something from me.

BERNARDA. Don't try to find out what. Don't ask about it and above all, never let him see you crying.

ANGUSTIAS. I should be happy and I'm not.

BERNARDA. So what's new?

ANGUSTIAS. Half the time I stare at Pepe through the window bars and he seems to fade away . . . as if he was vanishing into a cloud of dust kicked up by the herds.

BERNARDA. That's because you're in poor health.

ANGUSTIAS. I hope that's it.

BERNARDA. Is he coming tonight?

ANGUSTIAS. No. He went into town with his mother.

BERNARDA. Then we'll have an early night. Magdalena!

ANGUSTIAS. She's asleep.

ADELA, MARTIRIO *and* AMELIA *enter.*

AMELIA. It's so dark tonight!

ADELA. You can't see two steps ahead of yourself.

MARTIRIO. It would be a good night for burglars . . . or anyone else who needs to hide.

ADELA. The stallion was in the middle of the corral. White! Twice it's size, it filled up the darkness.

AMELIA. It's true. It was frightening, like a ghost.

ADELA. There are stars in the sky as big as fists.

MARTIRIO. This one stared at them till she nearly cricked her neck.

ADELA. Don't you like them?

MARTIRIO. I couldn't care less what's going on over the rooftops. I've enough to worry about with what happens inside these walls.

ADELA. Well that's typical of you.

BERNARDA. Of both of you.

ANGUSTIAS. Good night.

ADELA. Are you going to bed now?

ANGUSTIAS. Yes. Pepe isn't coming tonight.

ANGUSTIAS *exits*.

ADELA. Mother, why is it when there's a shooting star or a flash of lightning we say,

'Holy Barbara blessed on high,
Whose name is written in the sky
With paper and holy water?'

BERNARDA. The old ones knew many things we've forgotten.

AMELIA. I close my eyes so I won't see the lightning.

ADELA. I don't. I love it, fire flashing through a sky that's been dark and quiet for years.

MARTIRIO. But that's nothing to do with any of us.

BERNARDA. And it's better not to think about it.

ADELA. It's such a beautiful night. I'd like to stay up late and feel the breeze off the fields.

BERNARDA. But we have to go to bed. Magdalena!

AMELIA. She's in the middle of her first dream.

BERNARDA. Magdalena!

MAGDALENA (*annoyed*). Leave me alone.

BERNARDA. Get to bed!

MAGDALENA (*getting up in a bad mood*). You never give anyone a minute's peace!

She goes off grumbling.

AMELIA. Good night.

AMELIA *exits.*

BERNARDA. And you two, get to bed.

MARTIRIO. Why isn't Angustias's fiancé coming tonight?

BERNARDA. He's away on a visit.

MARTIRIO (*looking at* ADELA). Ah!

ADELA. I'll see you in the morning.

ADELA *exits,* MARTIRIO *drinks some water and goes out slowly, looking towards the corral doors.* PONCIA *enters.*

PONCIA. Are you still here?

BERNARDA. Yes, enjoying the peace and quiet, wondering where this terrible disaster you're sure is going to fall on my family might be hiding itself. I don't see any trouble Poncia.

PONCIA. Bernarda, let's just drop it.

BERNARDA. In this house there are no choices, no either or, no yes or no, there are only my eyes watching everything. They're the answer to every question.

PONCIA. That's true, on the surface of it that's very true. Your daughters live as if they've been stacked away in a cupboard. But neither you nor anyone else can watch what's happening in here. (*She puts her hand on her chest.*)

BERNARDA. They're breathing quietly enough.

PONCIA. Well that's what matters to their mother isn't it? Fine. I've got enough to do running round after you all.

BERNARDA. So you're keeping your mouth shut now, are you?

PONCIA. I know my place and I know how to keep the peace.

BERNARDA. The truth is you've got nothing to say. If there was grass on these floors you'd let the neighbours in to graze their sheep on it.

PONCIA. I keep the lid on more than you'd like to think about.

BERNARDA. Does your son still see Pepe at four in the morning? Are they still spreading their dirty lies about this house?

PONCIA. They don't say anything.

BERNARDA. Because they can't! Because there's no flesh here for them to sink their teeth into. And that's because I never close my eyes.

PONCIA. Bernarda, I don't want to talk about this because I'm afraid of what you might do, but you shouldn't feel so secure right now.

BERNARDA. I couldn't feel more so!

PONCIA. Lightning strikes in a moment. A clot of blood can stop your heart in a second.

BERNARDA. Nothing is going to happen. I know what you imagine but I'm on my guard now.

PONCIA. Well . . . Good for you.

BERNARDA. That's right.

The SERVANT *enters.*

SERVANT. I've finished the dishes. Is there anything else you want me to do Bernarda?

BERNARDA. No. I'm going to bed.

SERVANT. What time do you want me to call you in the morning?

BERNARDA. Don't. Tonight I'm going to sleep well.

BERNARDA *exits.*

PONCIA. When you can't stop the tide it's easier to turn your back on it and close your eyes.

SERVANT. She's so full of herself, she ties the blindfold over her own eyes.

PONCIA. I can't do anything. I tried to bring things to a head but I'm too frightened now. Can you feel the silence? There's a thunderstorm waiting in every room. The day it breaks it will sweep us all away. Well . . . I've said what needed saying.

SERVANT. Bernarda thinks no one can cross her. She doesn't understand the power of a man over a lonely woman.

PONCIA. You can't blame Pepe. Alright he was chasing Adela last year and she was crazy for him, but she ought to know better. A man is a man.

SERVANT. I've heard there were many nights he did talk to Adela.

PONCIA. That's true. (*Lowering voice.*) And not just talking with her.

SERVANT. I don't know what'll come of all this.

PONCIA. I'd like to sail across the sea . . . away from this battlefield, I'll tell you that.

SERVANT. Bernarda is speeding up the wedding plans. Perhaps nothing will happen.

PONCIA. It's too late. Adela could do anything and the rest of them hardly close their eyes.

SERVANT. Martirio as well?

PONCIA. She's the worst! That one is a well of poison. She knows she can't have el Romano. She'd take the world in her hand and crush it to dust if she could.

SERVANT. They're all evil!

PONCIA. They're women without men, that's all. When it comes to that, even blood counts for nothing. Shhhhh! (*She listens.*)

SERVANT. What's happening?

PONCIA (*getting up*). The dogs are barking.

SERVANT. Someone must have passed by the door.

ADELA *enters in her underwear.*

PONCIA. Aren't you in bed yet?

ADELA. I want a drink of water.

She drinks from the glass on the table.

PONCIA. I thought you were asleep.

ADELA. I woke up thirsty. Aren't you two going to bed?

SERVANT. In a minute.

ADELA *goes out.*

PONCIA. Let's go.

SERVANT. We've earned our rest. Bernarda won't let me stop all day long.

PONCIA. Take the lamp.

SERVANT. The dogs are going mad out there.

PONCIA. We won't sleep through that racket.

They both exit. The stage is almost dark. MARIA JOSEFA *enters with a lamb in her arms.*

MARIA JOSEFA. Little lamb, baby mine,
Let's go down beside the sea.
The little bug will be home and snug,
I'll give you my breast and my bread.
Bernarda, leopard head,
Magdalena, face of a hyena.
Little lamb,
Baaaa, baaa,
We'll gather flowers every hour at the gates of Bethlehem.
You and me don't want sleep,
We'll run out the door my little sheep,
And on the seashore we will hide
In a cottage made of coral.

Bernarda, leopard head,
Magdalena, face of a hyena,
Little lamb,
Baaa, baaa,
We'll pick flowers every hour at the gates of Bethlehem.

She leaves, singing, ADELA *enters again. She looks round cautiously then disappears through the doors leading to the corral.* MARTIRIO *enters by another door and stands, watching in anguish near the centre of the stage. She is also in her petticoats. She wraps herself in a small black shawl.* MARIA JOSEFA *crosses to her.*

MARTIRIO. Grandma! Where are you going?

MARIA JOSEFA. Are you going to open the doors for me?Who are you?

MARTIRIO. How did you get out?

MARIA JOSEFA. I escaped. Who *are* you?

MARTIRIO. Go back to bed.

MARIA JOSEFA. Now I know you. You're Martirio. Martirio the martyr. When are you going to have a baby? I've had this one.

MARTIRIO. Where did you get that lamb?

MARIA JOSEFA. I know it's a lamb. Why can't a lamb be a baby? Better to have a lamb than nothing at all. Bernarda, leopard head, Magdalena, face of a hyena . . .

MARTIRIO. Shhh! Don't shout!

MARIA JOSEFA. It's true. Everything is so dark. You think I can't have babies because my hair is white but I can, babies and babies and babies. This baby will have white hair and this baby will have another baby and that one will have another, all of us with snow white hair, we'll be like waves, one and another and another. And then we'll all sit down with our white heads and we'll be foam on the sea. Why isn't there sea foam here? There's nothing but black mourning veils here.

MARTIRIO. Be quiet! Be quiet!

MARIA JOSEFA. When my neighbour had a baby I'd take her chocolate and then she'd bring me some and that's how it was, always, always, always. You'll grow white hair but no neighbours will visit you. I have to go but I'm afraid the dogs will bite me. Will you come with me till I'm through the fields? I don't like fields, I like houses, houses with wide, open doors. The women and the children asleep in one bed, the men sitting outside on their chairs. Pepe el Romano is a giant. You all want him, but he'll devour you because to him, you're just grains of wheat. No, not grains of wheat. Frogs without tongues.

MARTIRIO (*pushing her*). Go on. Go back to bed.

MARIA JOSEFA. Alright, but then you'll let me out won't you?

MARTIRIO. Of course.

MARIA JOSEFA (*crying*). Little sheep, baby mine,
Let's go down beside the sea,
The little bug will be home and snug,
And I'll give you my breast and my bread.

She exits. MARTIRIO *closes the door behind her and goes to the corral door. There she hesitates but steps closer.*

MARTIRIO (*in a low voice*). Adela!

Pause. She goes closer to the door. She raises her voice.

MARTIRIO. Adela!

ADELA *enters. Her hair is dishevelled.*

ADELA. Why are you following me?

MARTIRIO. Leave that man alone!

ADELA. Who do you think you are?! Talking to me like that!?

MARTIRIO. That's no place for a decent woman!

ADELA. But how you longed to be there, didn't you?

MARTIRIO. Now I'm going to shout my lungs out. This has to stop!

ADELA. This is just the start. I'm strong enough to take what I want. I've got the strength and the looks you wish you had. I've seen death living here with us so I'm taking what's mine now, what was always mine!

MARTIRIO. That man has no soul in him. He came here for another woman. You're just throwing yourself in the way!

ADELA. He might have come for her money, but all the time his eyes are on me!

MARTIRIO. I won't let you have him! He's going to marry Angustias.

ADELA. You know as well as I do he's never loved her.

MARTIRIO. Yes.

ADELA. Yes, you know. You've seen it. He loves me.

MARTIRIO. Yes.

ADELA (*moving closer*). He loves me! *Me!*

MARTIRIO. Stick a knife in me if you have to but stop saying that now.

ADELA. That's why you can't let me have him. You don't care if he has a woman he doesn't love, well neither do I! He can spend a hundred years with Angustias for all I care. But you can't stand the thought of his arms around me because *you* want him. *You* want him!

MARTIRIO. Yes! Alright! Look at me! I'll say it without hiding my head under the sheets. I don't care if my heart bursts like a rotten pomegranate! I want him!

ADELA *hugs her impulsively.*

ADELA. Martirio! Martirio, it's not my fault!

MARTIRIO. Don't you touch me. You can't kiss the hate out of my eyes. There's the same blood in both of us but I don't care. I can't even try to love you.You're not my sister. You're just another woman.

MARTIRIO *pushes her away.*

ADELA. There's no cure for this. If you want to drown, you'll drown. Pepe el Romano is mine. He takes me into the rushes by the river . . .

MARTIRIO. I won't let you!

ADELA. I can't stand the horror of this place now I've tasted his mouth. I'll be whatever he wants me to be. Everyone in the whole village can turn against me. They can burn me with fingers of fire, they can chase me out, the hypocrites and I'll stand in front of all of them and put on my crown of thorns. I will be the mistress of a married man.

MARTIRIO. Shut up!

ADELA. Yes, alright. (*Lowering her voice.*) Let's go back to sleep. We'll let him marry Angustias. I don't care. I'll go and live in a little house, all alone and he'll visit me whenever he wants, whenever he feels the need.

MARTIRIO. It's not going to happen Adela, not as long as there's a drop of blood in my body.

ADELA. You're so weak. Right now I could bring a wild stallion to its knees with my little finger.

MARTIRIO. Don't raise your voice to me! I'm so full of hate now we're *both* going to drown, whatever I do.

ADELA. And they teach us to love our sisters. God must have pushed me out into the darkness because right now I'm seeing you as I've never seen you before.

A whistle is heard from the corral. ADELA *runs to the door but* MARTIRIO *stands in her way.*

MARTIRIO. Where are you going?

ADELA. Get away from the door!

MARTIRIO. Just try and make me!

ADELA. Get away!

They struggle.

MARTIRIO. Mother! Mother!

ADELA. Let me go!

BERNARDA *enters, she's wearing her petticoats and a black shawl.*

BERNARDA. Quiet! Behave yourselves! Oh if only I had a bolt of lightning in my fist!

MARTIRIO (*pointing at* ADELA). She was with him! Look at the straw on her petticoat!

BERNARDA. You've made a whore's bed in there!

She rushes at ADELA.

ADELA (*facing up to her*). Don't you shout at me! You're not my jailer any more!

She snatches away her mother's stick and snaps it in two.

ADELA. That's what I do with a tyrants rod! No one but Pepe can give me orders now!

MAGDALENA *enters.*

MAGDALENA. Adela!

PONCIA *and* ANGUSTIAS *enter.*

ADELA. I'm his woman! Do you know that now Angustias? Go into the corral and tell him you know. He'll be master in this house. He's out there now, breathing like a lion.

ANGUSTIAS. My God!

BERNARDA. The gun! Where's the gun!?

BERNARDA *rushes out, followed by* MARTIRIO. AMELIA *enters at the back, looking frightened, leaning on the wall.*

ADELA. You can't stop me!

She tries to leave, ANGUSTIAS *holds her back.*

ANGUSTIAS. You're not getting out of here with your skin gloating with pleasure. You stole him! You've shamed us all!

MAGDALENA. Let her go. Let her go somewhere where we never have to look at her again!

There is the sound of a shot. They all freeze. After a moment BERNARDA *enters carrying a gun.*

BERNARDA. Let's see if you dare go and look for him now.

MARTIRIO *enters.*

MARTIRIO. That's the end of Pepe el Romano.

ADELA. Pepe! My God! Pepe!

ADELA *runs out.*

PONCIA. You killed him?

MARTIRIO. No. He ran off on his mare.

BERNARDA. I can't help it. Women can't aim straight.

MAGDALENA. Then why did you say that . . . ?

MARTIRIO. To teach her! I'd like to pour a river of blood on her head!

PONCIA. You bitch.

MAGDALENA. You're possessed.

BERNARDA. Yes. But it's better if that's what Adela believes.

There is a noise off. She looks towards ADELA*'s room.*

BERNARDA. Adela! . . . *Adela!*

PONCIA *moves to the door.*

PONCIA. Open up now!

BERNARDA. Open the door! Four walls won't hide your shame, Adela.

The SERVANT *enters.*

SERVANT. The neighbours are up.

BERNARDA (*in a low voice, but roaring*). Open the door or I'll knock it down!

Pause. There's no sound.

BERNARDA. Adela! (*To* PONCIA.) Bring a hammer!

PONCIA *does so. She batters at the lock till the door gives. The others help.* PONCIA *forces her way through the door. She screams.*

BERNARDA. What?

PONCIA. May we never end like that.

The sisters fall back, the SERVANT *crosses herself,* BERNARDA *cries out and moves forward.*

PONCIA. Don't look at her!

BERNARDA. No. No I won't. Pepe you've run away with your life into the dark, under the trees but one day you'll fall.

Bring her to me! My daughter died a virgin. Carry her to her room and dress her like a virgin. No one say a word! She died a virgin. Tell them to ring the bells twice at dawn. Get her in! Quickly!

They drag ADELA*'s broken body into the house.*

MARTIRIO. She was happy a thousand times over. She had him.

BERNARDA. I'll have no tears! We'll look death in the face. Be quiet! (*To another weeping daughter.*) Quiet I said! You can cry when you're alone. We'll drown in a sea of mourning. She was Bernarda Alba's youngest daughter and she died a virgin. Do you hear me!? Silence, I said silence! Silence!

The End.